Marketing Skills

A Practical Guide

WITHDRAWN

WITHDRAWN

Garry Hynes &
Ronan Morris

MANAGEMENT BRIEFS

...ights for Busy Managers

Acknowledgements

We are indebted to Niall Treacy for helping to mould the shape of this book and for his careful reading and feedback at final draft stage. We would also like to thank the many people including David Behan and Michael Flanagan from Web Together who provided support and assistance during the production of this book.

We have drawn on Michael Porter's Five Forces Model and his ideas on the Value Chain. In the Chapter on Product we have taken inspiration from the work of Leyland Pitt in his book Marketing for Managers.

Also the various managers with whom we have had contact with throughout our careers, their input and insight is greatly appreciated.

We would like to particularly thank our editor Frank Scott-Lennon who kept us on track at all times and who was there with regular encouragement.

Finally, a special mention for our spouses, Stephanie and Grainne for their patience, support on this project and on all that has gone before.

Garry Hynes and Ronan Morris

November 2010

© 2010 Garry Hynes and Ronan Morris
ISBN 978-1-906946-03-6

Production credits
All design, art work and liaison with printers has been undertaken by
Neworld Associates, 9 Greenmount Avenue, Harold's Cross, Dublin 12. www.neworld.com

Publisher: Management Briefs, 30 The Palms, Clonskeagh, Dublin 14.

Table of Contents

Foreword

Garry and Ronan have provided within this book a very practical guide to Marketing Skills; the book will certainly help businesses to focus on their particular target market and put the building blocks of marketing in place within their organisations.

It is a very welcome addition to our developing series of Human Resource, Organisation Behaviour and General Management Books.

All of the books in the series aim to capture the essentials for busy Managers; essential knowledge and skill presented in an accessible and easy to read style.

A list of books already published within the series appears on the inside of the back cover. Also, on one of the last pages of the book, you will find a list of forthcoming titles which can also be viewed at our website www.ManagementBriefs.com.

We welcome any contact from you the reader; it will only improve our products and our connection to our reader population.

Frank Scott-Lennon
Series Editor
Frank@ManagementBriefs.com

November 2010

Introduction

1

Chapter outline
Introduction

→ The Scope of Marketing
→ The Marketing Roadmap
   - Really Understanding Your Market
   - Identifying Your Unique Offering
   - Bringing this Uniqueness to Life,
     Everywhere

Purpose of this Book

Most marketing books are written for marketers. This one isn't, in the strict sense. It does not take an academic approach to the subject. Its purpose is to provide you with an understanding that allows you to really engage with the marketing process, as it would be handled by marketers. It takes as its starting point the assumption that the reader has responsibility in, or oversight of, the marketing and sales effort of the company. That reader might be the Chief Executive, a General Manager, a Sales Manager, or the owner of a small business. Whatever category you may fall into you are likely to have recently come to the conclusion that you need a stronger awareness of the value of Marketing to a business.

The ideas and tools that this book will bring you through, are true for physical products as well as tradable services. So in the text of this book we use the words 'product' and 'service' interchangeably.

As customers use a wide range of sources of information about a product, there is also a significant benefit for all managers within a business to have a basic understanding of marketing processes. This will allow them to engage much more fully in the marketing plans and the impact of these plans on their department.

The Scope of Marketing

To have a successful business, you need customers who have a positive opinion of your product and hence choose it ahead of the competition. Generally the more people who have an increasingly positive opinion of your product, the higher your sales and profit margins. Creating this positive opinion of your product is not an easy task.

Customers build up a view of a product over time in a fairly unstructured and haphazard way. They are unlikely to be experts on the product, and hence they look for other signals or sources of information to help them make a decision. Will this product do what I need it to do? Will it be easy to use? Is it likely to break down or is it reliable? Is it made with quality components? Is it recyclable or produced from any recycled materials? Does the company behind the product have a good corporate reputation or have they been linked to activities that I don't agree with?

The list of variables that a customer might consider before choosing to buy your product is extensive and varies from category to category, country to country and customer group to customer group.

So what we all do in making decisions about what to buy, from corn flakes to cars, is rattle through our brains looking for pieces of information that help us get to a decision. These sources of information range from packaging design and advertising, through to childhood memories and associations.

Panel 1.1

Sources of Information

Much of marketing is simply an approach to trying to manage these sources of information in a way that influences customers in their purchase decision.

It is also about being able to dissect the marketplace into segments, amongst which the company can identify those that are most attractive to it in terms of opportunity for growth and profit. So, within Chapter 2, we will look at the process of segmentation and how it works.

We need too to understand what it is that motivates the customer (consumer or business customer) that we seek to sell to. What ticks the boxes for them? Is it one, or a combination of:

→ The reassurance the brand gives them?

→ Reducing their costs?

→ Improving their performance?

→ The price/value equation?

This book looks at ways of probing these issues and helping the user to a better grasp of the dynamics at work in the market.

Marketing tries to influence these sources by sending out a positive message about the product that the business believes will encourage them to buy. Getting the right message at every point of contact with a customer requires the whole business to get involved. The thinking and process behind this message may be led by a focused marketing campaign but because a customer is influenced by what he or she sees, hears or reads, everyone in an organisation can play a part.

The Marketing Roadmap

Marketing is an approach or a process for trying to influence the sources of information customers use before they make a purchase decision. It isn't a perfect process but when approached systematically, businesses can give themselves the best chance of having customers choose their product over the competition.

There are three basic steps within the marketing process:

❶ Really understanding your Market.

Really know your Product, your Customers (who exactly are you targeting and what's important to them) and your Competitors (what are they offering). We also need to address the issue of knowing where your company sits in the context of how influences in the wider marketing environment impact on your prospects for success.

❷ Identifying your unique offering.

This involves some analytical thinking about how the market is made up and where/how you can make a difference.

Think of your Product, Customers and Competitors as a Venn diagram.

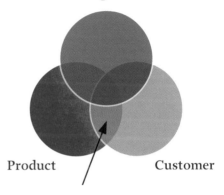

Competitors

Product   **Customer**

What is in the space that overlaps your Product and your Customer, but excludes your competitors that is most likely to drive profitable sales of your product? This is what is important to your customers; it is something that you alone deliver because it is not being offered by competitors.

❸ Bringing this uniqueness to life, everywhere.

Think of marketing as everything a company does from a customer's perspective. From the physical product, the packaging, the person at the call centre, (or the automated voice), the advertising, the price, the logo, the employees, or the offices. The great businesses deliver a consistent message around what makes them special for customers no matter where they come into contact with them.

Panel 1.2

Easyjet

Take the example of EasyJet in the context of these three steps

❶ Really understanding the Market

When Sir Stelios Haji-Ioannou was launching EasyJet in the UK in 1995, he knew he had to do something different to the big established airlines. He looked at who was flying and segmented them into key target groups. Business travellers didn't care a lot about price but wanted to be treated as VIP's, from special lounges and priority boarding, to quality meals and champagne on the flights. Family travel was predominantly package holidays with hotel and flight combined. What Haji-Ioannou learnt was that the vast majority of economy travellers really enjoyed going to new places. They see a trip as an adventure that brings them to a new place, full of possibility. Hence, what was important to people was where they were going, their destination. The flight itself was merely where they spent the time getting from A to B.

Looking at the competitors in the airline business, British Airways, British Midland and Air France, he saw that they were all charging hundreds of pounds per flight to pay for their very high levels of customer service. This high cost of airline travel meant that people could not afford to fly as often as they would like.

❷ What could make EasyJet unique?

EasyJet realised that if they could get rid of a lot of the 'extras' given to people before and during their journey, they could offer much cheaper flights to customers, profitably, and hence make it easier for them to travel more. They believed that since customers really wanted to travel to new places, they would sacrifice the 'extras' for the opportunity to travel more, due to lower prices.

❸ Bringing it to life

EasyJet looked at all the 'extras' and simply got rid of them. Then they went further. They:

→ looked at all the normal work practices and decided that if they cost money to deliver, they would eliminate them if they could.

→ they sold direct to customers cutting out the travel agents (and their commission).

→ they moved from telephone reservations in 1995 to internet booking in 1998 removing the need to employ reservations staff.

→ they created ticket-less travel, removing paperwork and got people to check-in online, removing the need to employ as many airport staff.

→ they got rid of the free food on flights removing a whole bunch of costs from food, to catering and management staff.

→ they drove this 'simple service model' at all levels, eliminating other unnecessary, complex-to-manage and costly services, such as pre-assigned seats, interline connections with other airlines and cargo/freight carriage. Even their logo and branding had a sense of low-cost about it.

→ they avoided anything that looked too corporate, traditional or extravagant because that was not what EasyJet was all about.

While the flying experience with Easyjet is very different from a flight with Virgin Atlantic and other airlines, as the fourth largest airline in Europe in 2008 with over 44 million passengers, EasyJet is hugely successful.

This volume is designed, amongst other essentials, to guide the reader through the same three-step process described above. In the early chapters we will look at some of the basics of getting the game plan off on the right footing.

From there we will move into the marketplace proper and ask, first of all, how it should best be segmented to make sense of different prospects within it.

Then, with those targets in focus the next question becomes, how does a company establish a competitive advantage for them? It is at this point that we will get down to what are often seen as the core components of marketing - product, price, promotion and place - referred to as the Four P's of the Marketing Mix.

Finally we will look at an approach to generating strategic options and formulating longer term plans.

Panel 1.3

Use of this Book

Best use of this book will come from:

→ Linking basic concepts and processes discussed to aspects of your own business

→ Isolating the bits that hold the best promise of improving your approach to Marketing in the short to medium term - rather than trying, initially, to build an all-embracing model

→ Then taking time to reflect on how some of the analytical concepts covered might help shape your longer term plans

Summary of Chapter 1

→ This book is aimed at 'non-marketers'

→ Marketing initially aims to manage the information flow to customers

→ Analyse, for your business, the Marketing Roadmap

- Really understanding your market

- Identifying the uniqueness of your product/service

- Bringing this uniqueness to life, everywhere.

Knowing Your Market

2

Chapter outline
Knowing Your Market

→ Segmentation - Dividing up the Market in a meaningful (to you) way so as to Reduce it to a Number of Defined Segments.

→ Target Marketing - Picking the Segments in Which You Choose to Compete.

→ Positioning - How, by the Characteristics of our Product and the Signals we send about it, do we get to Occupy a Unique Space in the Mind of the Consumer?

How much do you know, in terms of information assembled, about the buyers and potential buyers in your market? Without having some sort of organised view of this

→ you will be less than effective in your marketing effort;

→ you may be wide of target in your promotional effort,

→ you may be unaware of potential customers' existence.

But, with a comprehensive snapshot of the business landscape in mind, you are better placed to decide the areas within it that you are going after. We then look at how do you formulate an offer to those 'segments' that betters your chances of beating the competition.

Segmentation

Nearly every market is made up of customers whose needs differ and will not be satisfied by the same product or service. This creates opportunities for many companies to exist with similar offerings, but each with enough difference to attract their own unique customers. Slicing and dicing the market helps us get a clearer focus on the different types of offerings that attract customers and home in on areas that hold the most promise.

So let's look at different ways that you can approach segmenting your customers and help identify the ones that you should target.

❶ **Geographic:** For many companies this is the easiest place to start. Think of your organisation. If you are running a small newsagent then your customers are likely to be living locally. If you are a larger firm supplying building materials you may be able to target a larger region. Larger again and you may be able to target customers nationally or even internationally. The question you are asking yourself here is "where are the majority of my customers likely to be situated?" You may have customers outside this geographic area, this is fine, but where are the majority likely to be?

❷ **Demographic:** Demographic segmentation is about trying to compile a picture of different customer groups by such categories as age, gender, occupation and income. The implications of knowing your market in such terms are clear - on most main streets there are a number of pharmacies. Some are more geared to beauty products targeting a younger, female customer. Others will be more traditional where older male and female customers will feel more comfortable getting their prescription filled. Both shops offer a combination of medicines and beauty products but each has a very different main target customer.

So who are your customers? Can they be separated into different groups by age?

Are they more likely to be:

→ male or female?

→ office based?

→ travelling frequently?

→ working outdoors?

→ college educated or is education level not important?

Asking these questions helps you create a clearer picture of your target customer.

A traditional approach to demographic segmentation in Ireland has been the ABC1 Social Classification. So we see various publications claiming a percentage of AB (professional or managerial) or C1 (skilled working class) and so on through the ranks.

In the Business to Business (B2B) market the 'descriptors' are more about size of the target customers (number of employees, turnover), activity (process, assembly, services) and purchasing pattern (once-off, repeat).

❸ **Needs Segmentation:** Sometimes called Lifestyle Segmentation. This looks beyond the more basic approaches above and seeks to find out what it is your main targets want/need/ believe about your product category.

If we know what their activities, interests and opinions are we have a much more intimate picture of our customers, which makes

the task of formulating the offer and communicating it to them so much easier.

Panel 2.1

Lifestyle Segmentation

For example: bananas. At the basic level, it is very difficult to spot the differences between different types of bananas. Yet you can go into a Tesco store and be offered a choice of different bananas. There you may find:

→ a Tesco own-brand banana for the price conscious customer

→ a branded banana (Fyffes, Dole or Chiquita) for the customer who is looking for quality reassurance

→ a Fairtrade banana for customers who are concerned about treatment of farmers

→ an organic banana for the more environmentally conscious customer.

Each offering is targeting a similar customer (female, married with kids, etc.), yet very different based upon their interests and opinions.

So for your customers, what are they looking for more than the basic offering? Can you offer a more environmentally-friendly product? A product whose components are of higher quality? Can you offer greater reassurance that your offering won't disappoint, by adding an extended warranty, money-back guarantee or 24 hour technical support service? What do your customers need/want from you that you can deliver better than anyone else?

❹ **Leisure activities and interests:** Another popular approach to segmentation, consumer marketing, would be to classify people according to their leisure activities (e.g. listens to CD's, plays the lotto, eats out etc.). This can provide a really interesting insight into your potential customers that might help in the segmentation.

So for your customers, what are they looking for more than the basic offering?

Once we have specified the dimensions of the marketplace on some or all of these bases, the organisation now has to determine which segment(s) are most attractive in terms of:

→ Potential volume

→ Potential profit

→ Ease of access

→ Competition

→ Longer term viability

Having done that, the question now becomes: how well can we serve the most attractive segment or segments?

Panel 2.2

Segmentation Tables

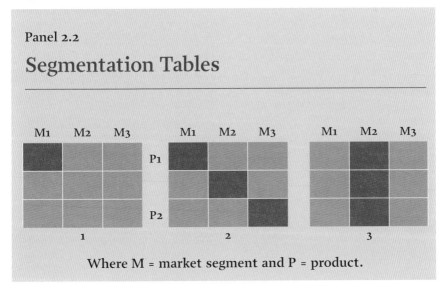

Where M = market segment and P = product.

The first table, in panel 2.2 shows a Niche Strategy, or concentrated marketing, where the player focuses on one particular segment, out of a potential nine, with a particular product/service. For instance Porsche selling a specialised prestige product, the 911, to a segment made up of high net worth individuals.

The second table depicts a strategy of marketing a product range across a variety of segments, which might be Toyota Motors selling a range of cars, from higher end saloons to mid-range, to the 'mini' category.

Table 3 could reflect the position of a large consumer products company, such as Unilever, marketing a variety of household and consumable products to the mid-market household segment.

Target Marketing

This might more appropriately be termed Marketing to the Target, because what it entails is formulating an effective Marketing Mix to focus on the chosen targets from the segmentation process. The task is to come up with the right combination of the Four P's of the mix - Product, Price, Promotion and Place (Distribution). These elements will be dealt with individually in more detail in Chapters 3,4,5 & 6.

Panel 2.3

The Marketing Mix

Product	Price
Promotion	Place

Within the wider Toyota stable, for example, all elements of the mix for Lexus differ distinctly (to the extent of having been set up as a separate company) from the main Toyota range. The product is upscale, the pricing reflects this, promotion, under a separate brand makes different appeals and the distribution is independent. In the main range the Prius and the Corolla, though similar in size and capabilities, really only share the element of place, or distribution. The Prius, with its hybrid petrol/electric engine, is a very different product. It is roughly a third dearer and the promotional/advertising appeal has a strong environmental tone to it.

So, are all of these equally important for you or do some of the four merit more attention than others? For instance, for Bentley cars the two that really matter are the Product itself and Place (the dealers they are distributed through); Price and Promotion are not as important.

Positioning

What we think of the product or service we offer is far less important than where we are in the 'mind map' of our customer. Perception is reality. Whatever the perception our target customer has of our offering, and of us as an organisation, is their reality. We may disagree. We may know our offering is superior to everyone else's in the marketplace. But this is irrelevant if we can't convince our customers.

Positioning is about **1)** starting with the target customer that we have identified through the segmentation analysis above and **2)** trying to build up an understanding of that target customer's view of us compared to our competitors.

Over time they have built up, mostly subconsciously, a perceptual map that places us in a position along with those of our competitors. The dimensions of their 'map' are not the conventional ones of longitude and latitude, but measures such as performance, price, prestige, reliability and so on.

Knowing where we stand in this landscape is vital to knowing what we can do to compete for the 'share of spend' by customers in our segment, i.e. how much they spend in total on magazines, on travel or whatever. By including competitor positions

we may also be able to discern gaps in the market.

Ideally the picture is built up through market research, but a thorough and honest appraisal, using sales experience and feedback from customers, can provide a workable alternative.

Often the simplest ways to gain an understanding work the best. Meet a customer or potential customer for coffee, explain to them that you are trying to look at ways of improving your offering and ask them for their suggestions. But don't try to sell to them. You invited them so they could help you. Let them talk and you listen.

Additionally, 'Google' your customers and your competitors. You would be amazed how much information is out there freely available. Just put a couple of hours aside and read websites, discussion boards, reviews etc.

If you are thinking of formal research, then talk to an expert. This is a specialised area and worth the extra expense of using an expert.

What we think of the product or service we offer is far less important than where we are in the 'mind map' of our customer.

→ If a gap exists, what is the size of the opportunity and what is the cost of entry? Is it big enough to make us money? Is it difficult or costly to reach (does it need much expensive new equipment, new patents, and so on?).

→ What do we need to do to reposition and move the perception of us along one/ both axes?

→ Should we be trying to compete directly with an entrenched category leader or should we look for more favourable competitive conditions in another niche?

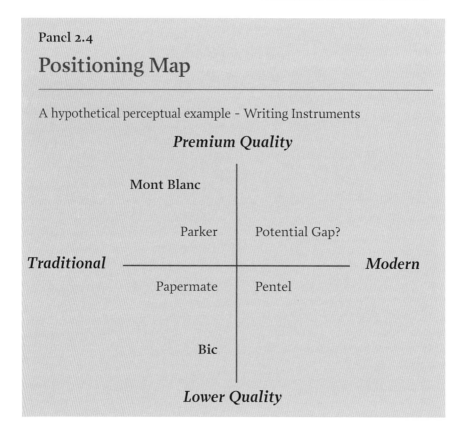

Panel 2.4

Positioning Map

A hypothetical perceptual example - Writing Instruments

Premium Quality

Mont Blanc

Parker

Potential Gap?

Traditional ———————————————— *Modern*

Papermate

Pentel

Bic

Lower Quality

Summary of Chapter 2

→ You must be familiar enough
   with the metrics of your
   marketplace - enough to drive
   the Segmentation of it

→ Know how to choose Target
   Segments that are the right
   ones to compete in

→ Know how to optimise your
   Positioning in the chosen
   segments, with particular
   reference to competitors.

3

The Product

Chapter outline
The Product

→ The Key Levels of the Offer:
  - The Core Benefit
  - The Tangible Product
  - The Augmented Product
→ The Product Life Cycle

We should restate here that the terms 'Product' and 'Service' are used interchangeably in this briefing - the principles discussed apply equally to both. In ways it may be better to think of the 'offer' that the firm makes in the marketplace. Indeed some offers are in fact a mix of product and service - a restaurant meal for instance.

At the end of the day this offer is what determines the firm's relationship with its customer. A flawed product erodes or destroys it; a superior service builds and enhances it.

The Three Key Levels of the Offer

❶ **The Core Benefit:** This is the basic satisfaction of need that the customer purchases, e.g.:

→ A power mower to cut the grass to an expected standard

→ Anti-virus software to block viruses from getting into your computer.

→ Petrol is bought for mileage on the road, not for the fuel in itself.

→ A Lotto ticket is bought in pursuit of a dream rather than as cold calculation of the odds of winning

The challenge with core benefits is that unless your offering is truly unique, it is likely that there are a number of companies offering products that deliver the core benefit. There are many different brands of lawnmower, many different companies offering anti-virus software, many locations where you can buy petrol.

Hence, Core Benefits are often the minimum standard required to do business.

The way to win business is to emphasise additional benefits either Tangible or Augmented.

❷ **The Tangible Product:** The actual features of the product and what they do for the customer:

→ **Product features:** The mower may have a two-stroke engine and a powertrain that drives the rear wheels. A mistake made by some firms, often technology/engineering driven where the dominant ethos may be in the technical excellence of those features, is to leave to the customer the interpretation of the benefit that the feature confers. Sometimes all or some of that benefit is lost in translation, so the message is - spell it out! For instance if the mower in our example has a cut-off feature that prevents the operator going near the blade housing with the motor running, the safety benefit of that technical feature should be highlighted in promoting the product. See panel 3.1.

→ **The Brand:** And all it conveys. What images and feelings, built up over time, about the product are evoked by the name, its logo if it uses one, the colour(s) associated with it?

In some cases the brand of a sub-component or supplier may be as important as the primary brand. The buyer of our motor mower may be impressed that it has a Briggs & Stratton or a Honda engine, P.C. users might insist on seeing the 'Intel Inside' logo, while coffee drinkers increasingly look for the 'Fairtrade' proof of origin.

→ **Quality:** What level of quality is appropriate for the target market? The answer is not always 'the highest possible'. If premium quality translates into premium prices, well and good, but if the buyer does not perceive it as added benefit, or is unwilling to pay the extra cost, there is a problem. The answer is to optimise quality for your market, erring slightly on the up-side.

Panel 3.1

Features and Benefits

A way to get to the <u>benefit</u> of your offering is to use the 'why?' technique. Ask yourself why do people buy from you, and keep asking 'why' until you get to what

(3.1 Continued)

you believe is the real benefit of your offering.

For example:

A customer buys anti-virus software. WHY?

→ Because they want to stop viruses getting into their computer. WHY is this important?

→ Because viruses can make computers crash and lose data. WHY is this important?

→ Because computers are at the heart of the business. WHY is this important?

→ Because business is stressful enough without having to worry about the computers going down at a critical time.

The feature is that the software stops viruses getting into your computer. The benefit is that the software provides peace of mind that your computer is safe as you focus on other more important priorities - so that is the benefit to sell to them.

❸ **The Augmented Product:** These, if you like, are the outer layer of satisfactions delivered with the product/service. Typically they only actually come into play after purchase.

→ **Warranty:** The guarantee that things will be put right in the event of failure has become an important differentiator in the market for consumer durables/capital items. Some car manufacturers, for instance, now offer 5 years (and more) parts and labour warranties with their models.

→ **Installation:** This has been particularly important in B2B marketing, but now increasingly so with consumers - e.g. P.C. software suppliers have learned that ease of installation is almost as big a factor with their customers as functional performance.

→ **After Sales Service:** The knowledge that there is some back-up if they hit problems (as distinct from warranty issues) is very important to vast numbers of P.C. users. Having a genuinely user-friendly website/help desk is a real competitive advantage issue for hardware and software suppliers. Household and Motor Insurers who rise to the test with a friendly and efficient claims helpline, build their reputation and brand at the expense of those who don't. Retailers who will accept no-quibble returns acquire a customer-focused reputation.

An important consideration with Augmented Benefits, is that they often are the reasons why customers may recommend you to others. Often these benefits kick-in when there is a problem, and dealing

with the problem efficiently and effectively can turn a customer into an advocate. Equally, dealing with a problem badly will make customers actively encourage others not to buy from you.

Panel 3.2

Augmented Benefits

Touchstone questions that need to be answered about product/ service offerings are:

→ How well does our core offer match the core needs of the people we aim to serve?

→ How does it stack up against the competition?

→ Do we, in the way we promote/present our offer, clearly get across the key benefits that its features provide to the customer?

→ Can we, in a cost effective way, find advantage over our competitors at the Tangible and/or Augmentation level?

The Product Life Cycle

All products and services go through a cradle to grave cycle. They are introduced, enter a growth phase, attain maturity and, finally, decline. Typically this cycle is shown as a curve of industry sales (not the individual company's) plotted against time. See panel 3.3.

Panel 3.3

The Product Life Cycle

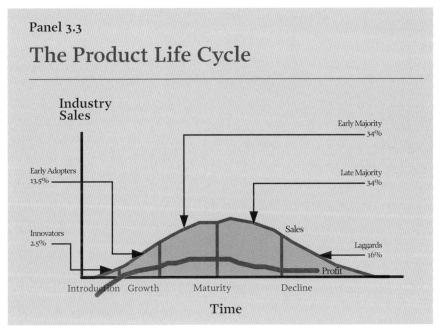

The shape of this curve will differ for various products. Two extreme examples would be:

→ Fads, such as the Rubik's Cube, would show a sharp spike, with rapid growth after introduction, an almost imperceptible mature phase and then phase out.

→ Baked Beans have been so long in mature phase that it is difficult to detect an obvious curve. At various stages Heinz and Bachelors have seen the beginning of decline and tried, successfully to counteract it with modifications (no added-sugar version, single serving microwave sizes, etc.).

Generally speaking however, the business you are in is somewhere along a curve akin to the illustration above and knowing where you are

along it can yield beneficial insight into what might be happening, and what might be done to capitalise on that insight.

❶ The Introductory Phase: The riskiest stage of all. Depending on which studies you read, anything from 60 to 85 percent of all new product introductions fail. The reasons are found mainly amongst:

→ There was no market there in the first place - the demand was conjecture rather than based on reasonable empirical evidence.

→ The target audience were not led, by promotional effort, to an insight into the benefits offered and how those benefits were a fit with their needs. Vigilant competitors on the sideline, or indeed from outside the industry, may then pounce on the new opportunity demonstrated.

→ The company lacked the financial resources to capitalise on a potential breakthrough with 'innovators' (the people who are first to try new things in a particular segment). Again this allows an opening to better funded competitors.

While this risk is a deterrent to many, others embrace it and, with imaginative and carefully harvested research and development, manage to beat the odds. Canon and 3M Corporation are examples often quoted.

❷ **The Growth Phase:** As the product gains acceptance and 'early adopters' begin, in volume, to take their cue from the 'innovators', the market enters a period of rapid growth. Characteristics of this phase include:

→ Gains in market share are relatively easily achieved. With a rising tide lifting all boats, advances are less obvious or not responded to vigorously. There is less pressure on pricing at this time.

→ New entrants are a feature. As the attractiveness of the business becomes apparent outsiders are drawn in. If the pioneering firm or firms have built good brand positions they will have some insulation against these.

→ A corollary of the above point is that this is the stage where eventual industry overcapacity has its roots. Individual projects, driven by the growth potential, fail to see the aggregate picture formed by all the projects in train. The golf course business in Ireland, Spain and Portugal among others looks like a prime example.

→ It is vital for a company to keep pace with the load that burgeoning demand places on procurement, production, distribution and after sales service.

❸ **The Mature Phase:** A majority of products are in this period of lower overall industry annual growth.

→ This becomes a real competitive battleground, with market shares being fought over as firms fight for expansion in a less buoyant market. One's gain in share comes from another's loss, so aggressive moves on promotion and pricing become the norm.

→ The share structure of the market (which companies have what percentage of it) has a big bearing on who dictates the plays. Those who come early to this stage, or establish a dominant share will have the biggest say. Others may be forced to adopt the role of followers, taking their cue from the leaders.

❹ The Decline Phase: As lower growth eventually, and inevitably, slips to no growth and then contraction, the questions become:

→ Is the decline terminal, or can fresh impetus, through product modifications or technological innovation, be injected into the market?

→ If the evidence is that decline has indeed set in, how can the company harvest the most from what remains with the minimum of effort and cost?

Panel 3.4

Guinness

An example of a brand here is Guinness, which has faced long term decline since the early 1980s. Yet, the company has continuously used innovation to slow the decline and in recent years bring the brand back into growth.

This innovation was a mixture of product innovation (Draught Guinness bottled, widget in the Can, Brewhouse series, etc.) and communication innovation with world class advertising and sponsorships. Interestingly, not all innovation worked but they demonstrated a willingness to continuously try new ways to strengthen the brand.

Summary of Chapter 3

→ Understand the Core Benefit you are offering to your customers and deliver this brilliantly.

→ Add value to your message by articulating the benefit in a way that makes it more tangible and relevant to your customers. Try the 'why?' exercise to help get to this tangible benefit (see page 21).

→ Seek ways to augment the benefits further by looking for additional benefits you can offer your customers (always keeping an eye to what the competition offers).

→ All products are part of a Product Life Cycle. Be aware of where you are on the journey and manage your business accordingly.

4 Pricing

Chapter outline
Pricing

→ Costs and Break-Even
→ Price and Quality
→ The Value Chain
→ Pricing Tactics
→ Win/Win Pricing

❶ Costs and Break-Even

It is sometimes said that pricing is too important to be left to the number crunchers and there's some truth in that. Certainly, in the normal run of events, you have to cover both fixed and variable costs - not doing so will in the long run lead to real problems for the business.

You may dip under the cost barrier for a very specific purpose, short term - running with a loss leader to attract customers to other offerings in your range or to gain entry to a market - but it is vital in such cases to know clearly what you are doing, why you are doing it and how long you are going to run with it.

Typically most attention tends to be paid to our costs and what the opposition is charging.

But cost-based pricing (e.g. total cost plus an arbitrary mark-up) in isolation is tunnel visioned and may obscure the reality of the marketplace.

Also matching, or closely shadowing what the competition charges, is almost to concede that you are in a commodity market where the only thing that matters is price. This takes focus away from what might be achieved, for example, by better positioning, promotion or service levels.

❷ Price and Quality

What is missing, too often, is a clear marketing driven connection between the price of the product or service and the customer value proposition that the company wants to support. Price is probably the element of the marketing mix that gets the least strategic attention and yet it has the propensity to drive or derail strategy. Consider for example the relationship in pricing strategy between price and perceived quality:

Panel 4.1

Price and Quality Table

		Price		
		High	**Medium**	**Low**
Quality	**High**	Premium	Good Value	Great Value
	Medium	Overpriced	OK Value	Good Value
	Low	Hit and Run	False Economy	Economy

So charging a price that is viewed by the customer (mainly by comparison with competitive offers) to be 'premium', is fine as long as your value proposition is also seen and experienced by them as top of the range. If your offer fails that test you run a serious risk of being seen as 'overpriced'. Recovering from that perceived (in their eyes) position, will be very difficult. Pricing decisions tend to have long term implications.

Another example would be that of a firm looking to enter a market, or to increase their market share, by means of a high quality offering at a medium price, but with a view to later increasing the price to competitor levels. Yes, this can and does work, but there are dangers. Potentially the biggest is that you get fixed in the consumers mind as the 'lower price' provider and they will resist or reject your price change. To pursue this strategy successfully you usually need to have some enhancement of the value proposition (e.g. 'New improved' or some further differentiation) to accompany the upward shift in price.

Pricing may be your best lever for profit. The underlying principle here is being able to assess the value that the customer puts on the service or product you offer.

❸ The Value Chain

In a business-to-business (**B2B**) context the best way to get to where price and perceived value are in equilibrium is to understand your customer's 'value chain'. This means knowing them so well that you can break up what they do into defined 'chunks' of activity:

→ Inbound - they buy in products and/or services. The better these meet their procurement processes (payment, quality assurance, storage, cost control etc.) the happier they are to pay a price for them.

→ Operations - they then do things with these purchases. They engage in assembly or processing to add value. The easier the purchased goods or services fit with their operations (e.g. by speeding them up, reducing costs/downtime, exceeding quality requirements), so much the better for the position of the supplier and the price they can ask.

→ Outbound - they package, store and deliver onwards their own value proposition. Can your input help at this point, e.g. by way of shelf life, ruggedness etc.?

→ Marketing and Sales - can the inclusion of a known and valued brand within their offer enhance their marketing efforts (e.g. in the way that Dell advertise that their P.Cs run with Intel microchips)?

→ Service - they back up all of this with after sales service, help desks or websites. Can you in some way supplement this effort (e.g. providing your own support service to assist with some queries/technical problems)?

While it may be easier to see where you might add value in their value chain at its earlier stages, every phase should be explored.

Panel 4.2

Marketing to Individual Consumers

Marketing to **Individual Consumers** often requires a different approach. Although many businesses have usefully applied the same value chain analysis, adapted from the B2B example above, it can be difficult. So you need to consider factors such as:

→ Price sensitivity: how likely is your customer to react to price changes? This may depend on whether they are buying for themselves with their own money or not, what proportion of their total spend on the category your product represents (e.g. of grocery basket), does it cost them to shop around for alternatives?

→ Differential pricing: is there variation in the way customers put a value on your service that would allow you to charge them different prices? Airlines do this very effectively, distinguishing for example between people who book well ahead and those who don't, between business travellers and holiday makers. So, you should know whenever they use your product differently or put a different value on its performance.

→ Emotions: buyers are not always totally rational about their purchases, so understand what your price says to them about your service. Some may require the emotional reassurance of a higher price, e.g. in healthcare products and services.

❹ Pricing Tactics

Ways of varying the price deal for different customers:

Discounts. The economics of costs will almost invariably mean that the more you sell the more margin you make, particularly if that comes in bulk orders from individual customers. So know the maths - how much to cut to provide the incentive to the customer and what levels of discount yield what profit for you?

Rebates. Rebating a proportion of the total paid when a customer reaches a target level of purchase can also have attractions. It may, for instance, preserve the impression that you are charging everyone the same price. It also has cash flow advantages, as you hold the 'discount' until the end of the period.

Extended credit. Preferred customers may be allowed longer credit. In a low interest rate environment the impact on cash flow is lessened, but one must always be aware that this approach may temporarily disguise underlying problems - such as your customers exposing you to a greater threat of default longer term.

❺ Win/Win Pricing

At the end of the day the objective should be to get the price right for both your company and the client. Neither the 'cost plus' or 'competition' approach to pricing will deliver this for you. Only a 'consumer demand' lead discipline will work. This means finding the 'price point' that is close to the most they would pay, but at which they are reasonably comfortable about the value they are getting. By doing this you are reassured on two fronts:

→ You know there was nothing more in it for you

→ You know you have not put unreasonable pressure on your customers' costs and thus avoid a potential build up of resistance.

Summary of Chapter 4

→ Know where your break-even point is

→ Know the range of competitors' prices.

But, since competing on price is usually the least attractive way of doing battle:

→ Use a Value Chain approach:

- inhabit your customer's mind

- find out what triggers satisfaction for them

- work on differentiations, positioning and promotions

- work also on the other elements of the mix (product, promotion, distribution) that nudge your value proposition in their direction at a price that meets both your needs.

5 Promotion

Chapter outline
Promotion

→ When to Promote Your Business
→ Active Promotion - Advertising
→ Models of How Advertising Works
→ Traditional Channels for Advertising

The third 'P' of marketing is promotion and it is the area of marketing that most people will be familiar with. Promotion is generally defined as communicating with the public in an attempt to influence them to purchase your products and/or services.

Some people incorrectly believe that advertising and promotion are one and the same. This is not the case as advertising is just one specific tactic that can be used to promote your business. There are many others that we will look at later.

For the purposes of this chapter we will look at promotion in its broadest possible context. We will mainly refer to products being promoted but it may be more relevant to you to consider services instead. It should also be remembered that often what is being promoted is the business itself or in fact the people within the business. For example, a professional services firm may want to communicate to the public about the expertise of particular individuals within the business.

❶ When to Promote Your Business?

Many businesses are too quick to engage in promotional activity. It is important to have an underlying strategy before you start any campaigns. As a starting point, you must be clear on where your product sits in the market, what are its key differentiating factors and what is your pricing strategy. The earlier chapters in this book should inform this process.

Passive Promotion

Even when you are not actively promoting a message about your business to the public your business is, simply by trading, still communicating with the public.

Every business should make a list of all of the potential contact points that the public has with the business. The public could be in contact with your business in any or many ways, see panel 5.1.

Panel 5.1

Interaction Points with Your Business

→ seeing the outside of your premises

→ walking into your premises

→ seeing your commercial vehicles

→ seeing one of your staff

→ talking to one of your staff

→ being left on hold waiting to talk to one of your staff

→ viewing your logo and stationery

→ touching your business card

→ visiting your website

→ visiting your toilets

→ purchasing from you

(5.1 Continued)

→ having a complaint dealt with by you

→ receiving a delivery from you.

Panel 5.2

Assessing how Your Business Passively Promotes Itself

Here are some examples of how a business can unwittingly communicate a less than perfect message about their business. Some of these may seem trivial but attention to this level of detail can pay huge dividends for business owners:

→ Telephonist has the volume too high/low on their phone. Either can be irritating for the customer

→ Reception is beautifully clean but is cluttered with old magazines

→ The customer interview room has other customer files thrown on the floor. One of the greatest sins!

→ Commercial vehicles that are not clean

→ The restaurant with the great dining area but with shabby toilets

(5.2 Continued)

→ Printing business cards on low grade paper.

When you have drafted your list, you need to then assess how your business promotes itself in each of these areas. See panel 5.2. You need to be brutally honest with this assessment, as this will provide the platform for your business to engage in active promotion campaigns. If you are unsure on any item, you should ideally refer it to someone unconnected with the business for an objective viewpoint.

Do not make the mistake of dismissing the importance of this analysis just because this type of customer communication is not directly revenue generating. Its importance lies in its *huge capacity to maximise the level and conversion rate of initial enquiries and also the level of repeat business that a business enjoys.*

Remember also that, unlike more active promotional activity, you have a greater level of control of results in this area.

❷ Active Promotion - Advertising

We are now going to deal with active ways you can communicate with the public about your business.

Advertising, in its various guises and through whatever channel, is a core feature of the marketing communications process. In fact

35

it is probably the first thing that springs to most people's mind at the mention of marketing. It's about having your message *received, understood and responded* *to* by your target audience. A good starting point for taking a look at how it works is to see it in the context of a communications schematic, such as:

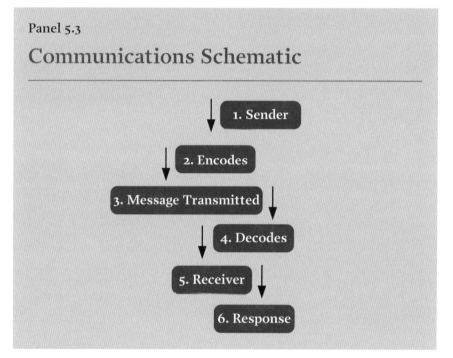

Panel 5.3

Communications Schematic

1. Sender
2. Encodes
3. Message Transmitted
4. Decodes
5. Receiver
6. Response

Distortion of the intended message, and the consequent failure to prompt the desired effect, is the big risk encountered at stages 2,3 and 4. It is where most wastage in advertising spend occurs.

So, from the outset the Sender must heed the advice offered in the chapter on pricing about 'inhabiting the customer's mind' as they encode their message to the intended target (i.e. the words and images, to be used). Conveying the features/functionalities of the product may be part of that so long as the benefits to the customer are clear (see Benefits vs Features on page 21). Do not leave it to them to join the dots. Don't allow the real value, to them, of your proposition be lost in translation.

If you are using an Advertising Agency, a written brief to this effect is vital. You know best *what* your customer values; the Agency's role is to formulate *how* to get that across to them.

You should also have a clear objective of what it is you want the advertising to achieve; is it:

→ A direct and measurable response?

→ Awareness and Brand building?

If it is the first of these, then there are a couple of models that have been used in advertising that are helpful as a type of checklist. Both look for a 'Hierarchy of Effects', bringing the target customer from a state of unawareness, through a couple of stages of engagement, to actually buying.

While this sometimes may seem to be asking a bit much of the advertising campaign, they do provide useful templates to pit the advertising proposal against. If, objectively, you cannot see the ads having a reasonable chance of carrying people along the continuum, there is probably something wrong with them. That could be, for instance, a creative deficit, using the wrong media or not enough spend.

It's about having your message *received, understood and responded to* by your target audience.

Panel 5.4

Models of How Advertising Works

Example 1

Attention	Interest	Desire	Action

This tasks the advertising with, firstly, getting the attention of the customer (otherwise you don't get out of the starting blocks), then sparking an interest in what you have to offer, followed by a desire to acquire the product and, finally, acting upon that wish.

A second standard of measurement that has stood the test of time would be the DAGMAR model.

(5.4 Continued)

Example 2

| Unawareness | Awareness | Comprehension | Conviction | Action |

Very similar in ways to the previous model, but with slightly different stage points. So, the question is, will the ad make someone aware of your proposition, will they properly understand the benefits it pitches to them, will they believe the claims made and will they actually buy?

Either of these models gives us a useful litmus test for any proposed advertising campaign.

Whilst few would pass every stage with flying colours, if it can be objectively felt that a reasonable proportion of the target segment could be 'nudged' along the spectrum, then that may be all you can ask for. Certainly if you can see an obvious break in the chain, questions have to be asked about the nature of the advertising proposal.

Panel 5.5

Awareness and Brand Building

If the objective is Awareness and Brand Building a slightly different set of criteria come in to play.

Some awareness advertising is short-term. It is high impact and often used to trumpet awareness of new entrants into markets such as mobile phone and internet service providers. But much of what we are talking of here has longer term ambitions. It is about building the image of the brand and positioning it in relation to the competition. So does the advertising support the context that the company wants its product to be seen in? Does it evoke, in the minds of present and potential clients the image/personality they want to project (the Corporate Image)?

For example, that might be:

→ For Audi cars - engineering prowess

→ For L'Oreal cosmetics - luxury at a price

→ For Lyon's Tea - pure quality.

(5.5 Continued)

Companies spend large sums of money, over time, to build and protect this 'value' in the customer's mind. It becomes a valuable asset to the company. So, for instance when Unilever bought a majority shareholding in Lyon's Tea in the mid-90's they were willing to pay way over the conventional book-asset value in order to bring the brand leader in the Irish market into their own range of consumer offers.

❸ Traditional Channels of Advertising

While the traditional channels of communication, such as TV, radio and the printed media, are losing quite heavily to the internet, they still attract a significant chunk of advertising spend and have their own distinct advantages.

Television: Very much a mass market option, TV has the advantage of combining visual with sound and motion to appeal to the senses. Up until quite recently production costs and the cost of exposing the ad were high so this option has only been feasible for businesses with larger budgets.

The arrival of satellite TV and the multitude of new channels that now come into our living rooms has moved this medium more within reach of many business owners. There are two key reasons for this:

Cost. While the overall cost per viewer remains largely the same, the fact that some TV stations have much smaller viewer figures allows smaller advertisers to test response rates for ads without incurring huge cost. In addition, there is a growing acceptance that lower cost but high quality graphic ads can, in some cases work just as well as ads shot with broadcast quality video.

Targeting. With more TV channels comes more program choice and this means a much wider variety of programming with almost all niche tastes being catered for. If you have a product or service that appeals to one of these niches, TV advertising could offer a cost-effective way to get at your key audience.

Radio: A lower cost option with more opportunities for localisation and targeting of audiences. But, with only sound to work with and a lower (than TV) attention level in the audience, creative impact is at a premium. Without a stand-out jingle, engaging humour or attention grabbing catch phrase the message will be lost in the background noise.

Another issue with radio advertising is that research tends to suggest that a fair degree of repetition is required in order to get your message across effectively. That's why you will tend to see radio ad packages being sold in bundles of 'spots' that are normally fairly close together. This can make radio advertising very costly - at least when done on a national station. If your budget is limited it may be better to concentrate on getting the right level of repetition on one or more local stations rather than having a very scattered campaign on a national station.

Getting some creative input with your ad is also very important. It is unusual for an amateur script to 'cut through' in this media. This adds to your cost but may improve the recall/response rates to the ad.

Radio advertising has also suffered in recent years from the growing numbers of music listeners who choose to listen to their music on MP3 players, thus avoiding advertising messages from radio. This is particularly the case in the younger market segment which had always been a key strength of radio advertising. Amongst older age groups, listenership figures remain very healthy.

Print Media: Ideal when more detail is required in the message, since the target, once drawn to the ad, has the choice of how much time to spend reading (even re-reading) it. Again, the creative task is to get and keep that attention. It is relatively low costs and has good segmentation production opportunities.

National newspapers offer huge reach but are usually beyond the budget for smaller business owners who tend to instead focus on local newspapers.

Local newspapers tend to have a more flexible approach to pricing so you will need to negotiate the very best deal for your business. A long term commitment to the newspaper should secure you a sizeable discount and allow you get the best spaces in the paper. Unless you are targeting a special section of the paper, you should always ask for as 'early' a position as possible. Front page will always be more expensive while 'early' right positions (pages 3,5,7 etc) will be next best. Right side is favoured as most people tend to look at the right side first. Back page can seem an attractive option but it depends on the paper. It's therefore a good idea to know the paper you are advertising in. If you don't, you should buy a few copies and then decide what positions would best suit your ad.

Bear in mind also that local newspapers will be more positive towards any public relations (PR) material that you send to them if you are an active advertiser, whereas national newspapers will more strictly separate advertising and editorial departments. PR will be taken up in more detail within our next chapter.

The last issue to consider with newspapers is that average readership levels continue to fall every year as more and more people source their news (for the moment, free) from the internet. This has been particularly damaging for national newspapers but less so for local newspapers.

Summary of Chapter 5

→ Passive promotion is the platform that active promotion should be based upon.

→ Don't spend your money actively promoting your business until you are convinced that you will be able to meet or exceed the expectations of the customers that you end up attracting.

→ AIDA = Attraction - Interest - Desire - Action

→ DAGMAR = Unawareness - Awareness - Comprehension - Conviction - Action

→ The relative value of the more traditional advertising methods has diminished but they are now more accessible for small businesses:

  - TV

  - Radio

  - Print Media

6

Other Promotional Methods

Chapter outline
Other Promotional Methods

→ Ambient Advertising
→ Direct Marketing (DM)
→ Internal Marketing
→ Public Relations
→ Exhibitions and Trade Shows
→ Networking
→ Sponsorships

➊ Ambient Advertising

This is one of the newer forms of advertising. So much so, that there is much confusion as to the exact definition of 'ambient advertising'.

In most definitions, reference is made to the non-conforming nature of the location of the advertisement. Others also mention that the advertisement itself is often non-conforming and unusual in nature. Where confusion arises is when a form of advertising which was once considered ambient is used so frequently that it is no longer considered unusual and becomes mainstream. An example of this would be advertising on the sides of buses. For the purposes of our discussion, we will assume that if a particular medium started out as 'ambient' then it will always remain so.

> We will assume that if a particular medium started out as 'ambient' then it will always remain so.

The one slight problem with this approach is that we should include billboard advertising within 'ambient' even though the use of billboards probably predates the use of the word 'ambient' in relation to advertising.

Panel 6.1

Ambient Advertising Options

→ Exterior vehicle advertising (buses, taxis, commercial vehicles)

→ Interior vehicle advertising (buses, taxis, trains)

→ Billboards (Large 48 sheets, bus shelters, mobile billboards)

→ Back of till receipts

→ Petrol stations (back of petrol pumps, TV ads near pumps)

→ Posters in customer toilets

→ Beer mats

→ Pedapods (roofed bicycle that can accommodate passengers)

→ Floor advertising

→ Carrier bags

→ Car park barriers.

Ambient advertising has grown in popularity in recent years. Reasons for this include:

→ Traditional advertising costs have risen in relative terms

→ Audiences for traditional forms of advertising have diminished

→ The increasing levels of advertising 'clutter' that the average consumer is exposed to.

With these trends set to continue, it is likely that ambient advertising will continue to grow.

The key advantages of this form of advertising are:

→ The ability for the advertiser to get close to the point of sale and therefore more directly target consumer needs

→ They can be very cost effective when compared to promotions that focus on price reductions

→ They can also generate PR for your business.

Panel 6.2

Successful Ambient Campaigns

Examples of successful ambient campaigns include:

→ Volkswagen using the back of petrol pumps to promote the fuel efficiency of their cars

→ Diageo using mini-drinks menu in bars to promote the sale of high value drinks such as hot whiskeys, Irish coffees etc.

(6.2 Continued)

→ At Venice Airport, a local casino converted a baggage carousel to look like a roulette wheel.

When should you consider using ambient advertising?

For most small businesses it may not be possible to justify the cost involved for a full campaign based on a new media such as this. However, for some businesses this can be a very effective advertising medium. Normally, the campaigns that work the best are ones that make best use of the advantages of the medium, in particular in relation to the proximity to the point of sale. For example, an advertisement for a new restaurant on a bus shelter situated close to the restaurant.

❷ Direct Marketing (DM)

DM is a sub-discipline within marketing. It differs from traditional forms of marketing in two key ways:

→ The marketing communication is sent directly to the consumer without the use of an advertising medium such as TV or radio. The most common methods include direct mail, e-mail and telemarketing

→ The communication is usually designed to elicit a 'direct' response from the customer to the advertiser. Usually by way of a freephone number, reply-post envelope or invitation to visit a website.

Panel 6.3

DM and Small Business

Small businesses are usually attracted to DM for one or more of the following reasons:

→ Usually they are quite easy to put together. A campaign might consist of a letter or an email or a simple flyer

→ They suit limited budgets as production costs tend to be quite low

→ Monitoring of results is relatively straightforward

→ Even if you don't have customers to communicate with, it is possible to buy lists of customers from list brokers.

The downside of DM is that it can be difficult to attract the attention of your intended audience. Your DM communication could be just one out of a hundred targeted at that consumer that week. As more and more businesses advertise in this way, the average success rate appears to continue to fall.

One way to mitigate this risk is to invest more money in your DM campaigns by taking on advice in key areas. This could mean having a brochure professionally designed to go with your letter. You could also hire a copywriter to draft the text for that brochure and for your letter. Adding a special offer to attract customers is another way of boosting response rates. For telemarketing, professional scripting of outbound telephone calls can greatly improve response rates.

DM's reputation also suffers with poor targeting. Some businesses are lazy in their targeting efforts and can be less than accurate when manipulating customer databases for DM campaigns. A campaign that is poorly conceived and executed can seriously damage the brand of the advertiser.

Panel 6.4

Tips for DM

→ Keep your database up-to-date and avoid using very old customer lists.

→ If you believe that the address data is poor, pay to have it fixed up by a data cleaning company.

→ Test your communication out on a focus group before sending it to actual prospects or customers.

→ Always give your audience the chance to easily opt out of future communications, (e.g. by ticking a box). This saves you time, money and effort!

(6.4 Continued)

→ Monitor your results. This means specifically recording the number of enquiries and sales generated by each campaign.

❸ Internal Marketing

This is the simple idea that whatever you are doing externally in marketing, you should be communicating your plans in great detail internally in your business.

We all have experience of getting a special offer in the post from an advertiser and then calling the business in relation to it only to find that the employee on the other end of the telephone knows nothing about the offer. How bad does that business look? That is a very simple example showing the effect of a simple piece of information not being communicated.

At a higher level, it is important and valuable to get input from employees in relation to marketing strategy. The advantages of this include:

→ Your employees sometimes have information about your business that you don't - they can help you!

→ Employees can help with targeting efforts such as adding and subtracting customers from a database.

→ Marketing campaigns should bring new customers and this can cause spikes in demand for your product/service. Involving employees in the process will minimise any issues caused by this.

→ Good internal marketing can also improve co-ordination between business functions.

→ Negates some of the trip wires described on page 34

→ Employees are encouraged to offer superb service to customers to ensure the success of campaigns.

→ Non-marketing staff are given an understanding of the discipline and how it can positively influence business performance.

→ Creates a better general understanding of the business amongst employees.

❹ Public Relations

Achieving favourable publicity through the media is one of the most cost effective forms of promotion you can get for your company, because it has two great advantages:

→ It is usually much cheaper than paid-for advertising

→ It carries more credibility than paid-for advertising.

A good starting point is to remember that the media need news and stories to survive, but that many competing voices are vying for their attention, so getting your message and timing right is critical. Regional or local exposure will naturally be easier to get than national.

47

Success in this area is down to careful planning, timing and perseverance. While it does not necessarily mean employing outside help, that may be worth consideration.

Panel 6.5

Clarity of Objective

Be clear about what your objective is. For example, is it about:

→ Generating general goodwill about the company amongst customers or the community or some other target audience?

→ Publicising a specific event, a product launch, branch opening, a trade award?

→ Attracting sales leads?

→ Countering negative publicity?

→ An integrated programme over time covering several of these?

You need to establish clearly who your target audience(s) are. Who do you want to get to with this campaign and what are the key messages you need to convey to them? Here good advice might be to adopt some of the pointers given under the advertising section. So:

→ pick your target segment carefully,

→ go at them with a core USP (Unique Selling Proposition)

→ do not dilute your argument with a raft of supplementary claims, things you think it might be nice to say while you're at it.

By all means support your message with facts, findings, quotes etc., but stay on message without cluttering it.

Now you need to decide what vehicle(s) are to be used to carry the communication and who to direct it to. So know who the people are in the press, TV or radio, who handle news, features, business, or whatever is appropriate to the circumstances and address yourself exclusively to them. Using a scattergun approach in the hope of success is not good PR management.

Press Release: If you are taking this route to publicising some event/milestone, timing is of utmost importance. Get it out while the news is hot - old news is no news. Also get the release to the media to suit their time of going to press/air (you can send it early with an 'embargo' time and date). Always include a contact name and number, available not just in your office hours.

→ Make it as succinct as possible - if they want more detail they will get in touch.

→ A good headline is half the battle, followed by an absorbing first (short) paragraph. Promote without exaggerating.

→ A photo greatly improves your chance of being taken up.

Make sure it integrates well with other marketing and sales activities; above all make sure there is no conflict or contention.

Interview: Offering the media someone for interview has the potential for great impact, but it all hinges on having the person with the right combination of knowledge of the subject, confidence and ability to think on their feet. Remember you lose much of the control that you have in the press release. This is especially true if it is live on air, but also in the case of an interview with a newspaper or magazine - you will not have any say in what is eventually published.

Panel 6.6

Tips for PR

→ Establish clear objectives for your PR effort:

→ Know your target audience and what they read/watch/ listen to

(6.6 Continued)

→ Craft your message and deliver it in appropriate channels

→ Think through, how will we know if this has worked?

❺ Exhibitions and Trade Shows

Depending on the type of business, exhibitions and trade shows can be a cost-effective way of generating new leads for your business.

Usually this form of advertising tends to work best where either:

→ Your product fits very well with the particular theme of an exhibition. For example you make picture frames and you show your products at an art exhibition.

→ Your product is quite novel or has a unique broad appeal. For example a new robot vacuum cleaner could be displayed at various different types of exhibitions.

Depending on the type of business, exhibitions and trade shows can be a cost-effective way of generating new leads for your business.

Panel 6.7

Tips for Exhibitions and Trade Shows:

Before committing to a space at an exhibition, you should consider all associated costs including the cost of hiring the space, staff costs, cost of buying or hiring stand, cost of posters and other display material, free giveaways, travel costs etc.

→ If you can't afford a good quality display you should probably opt out.

→ When deciding how much to spend on display material, consider how often it might be re-used.

→ Study the map of the exhibition very carefully before deciding which space to choose. Watch out for likely areas of high traffic, spaces near popular stands, etc. Seek advice from experts if you are unsure.

→ Record all enquiries and follow up within 1-5 days following the show.

→ Leave time for yourself to look at other exhibits. There may be opportunities to network in order to create synergies with other businesses targeting the same types of customers.

→ Arrive early to give yourself as much time as possible to set up.

→ Resist the temptation to pack up early.

❻ Networking

While many business owners may not see this as being a genuine promotional activity, networking is indeed about promoting yourself and, by connection, your business. You may also find it appropriate to encourage other staff members to network.

Panel 6.8

Different Forms of Networking

There are many different forms of networking. Some examples include:

→ Getting to know businesses local to your own business

(6.8 Continued)

→ Getting involved with local Chambers of Commerce

→ Joining industry bodies

→ Joining local sports clubs

→ Joining recognised business networks that share leads among members

→ Online business networking clubs such as LinkedIn

Some business owners are uncomfortable with the social element of networking. It can be difficult to establish yourself within a new group. Here are some practical tips that might help:

→ Many people struggle with coming up with a good 'opening line' for when they meet someone new. We recommend the following: "Hi, I'm ‹‹your name››", and see where that takes you.

→ If you enter a crowded room, try to assess the body language of the various groups that you want to join in with. Some groups will be closely huddled, subliminally sending a message that they do not want more participants. Other groups will look more 'open' and will be sending out the opposite message.

→ Try to ask questions of the person(s) that you are talking to. Eventually, you will get the opportunity to talk about yourself (and your business).

→ Try not to mention the title of the job that you do, try instead to talk about the effect of your work. For example, if you are an accountant and are asked what you do, you could say "I save people money". This approach works on two levels. Firstly, it's more interesting and secondly it leads to a series of supplementary questions. In this case "Oh really? How do you do that?" "Tell me more about that" etc.

→ If someone hands you a business card, you should read it immediately and make it obvious that you are doing so. It is a common courtesy but often forgotten. You should also pass back your own business card.

→ You should be dressed appropriately. Always err on the side of being overdressed as opposed to underdressed.

→ Have a clear idea of the types of people you want to talk to, the ones that could be valuable to your business. If the person you are talking to does not fit your profile you need to find a polite way to move on to someone else.

❼ Sponsorships

One area where most small business owners are inundated with options is in the area of sponsorship. It is an area that can provide the best return on investment but can also end up as being a complete waste of money.

Small Business and Sponsorship

For small businesses there are three types of sponsorship:

→ 'Blackmail' sponsorship - your best customer asks you to buy a tee time for four people and sponsor a hole at a local golf classic. You know that the exposure for your business will be very limited but you can't let your best customer down. This is normally just treated as a necessary cost of doing business.

→ Local club/association sponsorship - this is where there could be a genuine element of exposure for your business to customers within your target segment. These opportunities should be assessed on their merits. Often they can represent tremendous value for money. In particular where you take the time to negotiate the very best arrangements in relation to signage, special mentions etc. These sponsorships can create significant goodwill for a business.

→ Media sponsorships - this is where the business, for example, sponsors a radio show or the weather forecast. Or it could also be the sponsorship of a particular section of the newspaper. Again, these should be assessed on their merits as they can represent great value. This is because there can be less competition for this type of advertising. It can be particularly suitable if your product or service is difficult to explain in a normal radio or press ad and where you are simply looking to get the name of your business mentioned.

Summary of Chapter 6

→ There are many different ways to promote your business; some require an investment of money, others an investment of your time

→ Ambient advertising - relatively new and promising for many businesses

→ Direct Marketing - cost effectiveness depends on good targeting

→ Internal Marketing - make sure your employees are aware of all marketing efforts

→ Public Relations is a key process for getting the message to your market

→ Exhibitions may be an option for certain businesses

→ Sponsorships and how to manage them.

7 Online Marketing

Chapter outline
Online Marketing

→ Websites
  - Common Mistakes
→ Search Engine Optimisation (SEO)
→ Link Baiting and Blogging
→ Search Engine Marketing (SEM)
→ Banner Advertising
→ Social Media
→ Permission Marketing - Email Marketing
→ Information Marketing
→ Offline Integration
→ The Growth of Online Marketing

This form of advertising is quite unique in the way that it has almost levelled the playing field when it comes to small businesses advertising against big businesses. Yet, there are many small business owners that have yet to fully appreciate the value of this new medium and how it can be central to growing their business.

Another unique aspect of this form of marketing activity is that it is relevant to almost every trading business. There are a very small percentage of businesses that firstly would not benefit from an online presence and secondly would not benefit from promoting this presence.

❶ Websites

The starting point for most businesses is to have a website. A website can operate on one or more levels for a business such as:

→ Providing basic information for consumers (basic brochure website)

→ Showcasing the products and services offered by the business (advanced brochure website)

→ Selling the products and services offered by the business (e-commerce website)

Each business needs to decide the appropriate site for them.

You may already have a website or you may be thinking about having one built. A very practical way to give advice in this area is to highlight the common mistakes made by small businesses when investing in an online presence.

Common Mistakes

→ **The website is dealt with as a standalone project.** The effect of this mistake is that the website often ends up not being consistent with the offline messages being communicated by the business.

→ **The cheapest provider is selected.** As is the case in many areas of business, you usually get what you pay for. Having no website is nearly always better than having a poor website. Only select web design companies that have a portfolio of completed websites that show that they are appropriate for your project. Also note that the cheapest website usually ends up being a false economy as it needs to be replaced within a short space of time.

→ **The brief given to the web design company is poorly drafted.** As the business owner, you will know more about your business (its products, the competition, the market etc.) than anyone else and significantly more than the person employed to design your website. Your task is to get this knowledge out of your head and on to paper in a way that the web designer can understand so that they in turn can develop a website that actually delivers value for your business.

→ **An insufficient budget is allocated to the project.** Often businesses will set aside a budget that is equivalent to the cost of the design and print of a corporate brochure on paper. This is a mistake and here is why:

- The corporate brochure will have a much shorter shelf life than the website

- The website is very flexible and can be changed at short notice to reflect changes to prices/products/services or to suit market conditions

- Usually, the website will attract significantly more 'eyeballs' than any corporate brochure

- The website is much more customer-friendly in that it is interactive. Customers can choose the information that they want in the order that they want as opposed to the paper brochure where it is presented in the format and order that the business owner wants.

Neither author of this book has yet encountered a business that claims to have spent too much on their website. This should illustrate the importance of getting the budget right from the outset.

→ **The website is too focused on providing information.** The basic brochure website approach can work for some businesses. This means providing the bare minimum information that a customer might want to find out about your company e.g. opening hours, brief history, location map, list of products. However, most businesses can and should be more aggressive than this when it comes to promoting their business. Think of it this way: a visitor to your website is likely to be interested in becoming a customer. However, if they are surfing the web, they may also be looking at your competitors' websites. You need to make sure that as many of these 'prospects' become customers. To do this you need to offer a little more. This might include one or all of the following:

- Better presentation of information about the products/services provided e.g. high resolution photos of products

- Appropriate biographies of key personnel in the case of service providers

- Compelling reasons why they should deal with your business

- Simple online enquiry forms

- Special features to help them access information more easily/quickly

- Contact us e-mail address

→ **Finally, no follow up budget is allocated to marketing the website.** As part of the website project there needs to be a clear plan showing how traffic will be driven to the new website and a budget needs to be allocated for same. Some of the most used methods for generating traffic are mentioned below.

The above six mistakes (and others too!) continue to be made and they are mainly made by small and medium sized businesses. The reason for this in many cases is down to a lack of understanding of the value of and the workings of the Internet. It is imperative that where there is a lack of understanding that help is sought in this area. This could mean engaging a marketing or technical consultant to help out on a project.

This next section assumes that your website is in existence and that it needs to be marketed effectively. The six methods listed below can each play a role in ensuring that traffic to your website is maximised but in a cost-effective way.

❷ Search Engine Optimisation (SEO)

At a minimum, your web design company will normally ensure (but you should still check) that your website is registered with all of the main search engines i.e. such as Google, Bing and Yahoo. This means that these search engines will at least look at (trawl) your website in response to searches that are requested by visitors to the search engine websites.

Panel 7.1

Search Engine Variables

→ Number of links to your site (where another site links to your site)

→ Page titles on relevant pages

→ Relevance of the text (does the text mention the search terms and/or associated key words?)

→ Position of the text on the page (Look at what is visible on a standard monitor when your page loads. Generally speaking, the search engines will place a higher value on the text within this area.

Panel 7.2

Example : A Search Engine Result

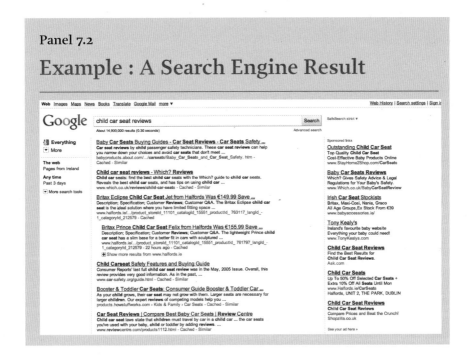

However, there are a wide number of variables (see panel 7.1 above) that decide in which order the search engines present their results. Most businesses will want their site to feature as high as possible for search terms that are relevant to the business. The conventional wisdom is that you really need to appear on the first page and ideally in the top five on page 1 of the results so that your business website is immediately visible. In certain sectors these top positions are highly sought after and competition for them can be fierce.

It is important to understand that it is not just your homepage that is optimised as the search engine can bring up any one of the pages on your website as a potential result.

The best time to deal with your SEO requirements is when your website is being built. At the initial design stage, an experienced web development company will assess and then implement your SEO requirements. If you have engaged a competent web development company you may never need to do further SEO work on your site.

However, you may have an existing site and it is possible that the SEO effort may not be up to the required standard. There may then be a requirement for an experienced web professional to come in and look at fixing any SEO issues that were not initially dealt with at launch stage.

Panel 7.3

SEO Examples

The requirement for SEO investment also varies greatly from business to business. Here are two examples showing two different businesses and their specific SEO needs:

Example 1:

→ Boutique in a London suburb (say Bromley) selling maternity wear

→ Customers mainly within 15-mile radius

→ Only one competitor has a website

→ Likely search terms: 'maternity wear Bromley', 'maternity shop Bromley', 'maternity boutique'.

Assessment: Even a reasonably well designed website will ensure that this business appears on the first page of search engine results. There is a low level of competition and the geographic target area is relatively small.

Example 2:

→ Mortgage broker in Dublin

→ Targeting customers throughout the city

→ Lucrative business sector with many competitors

→ Likely search terms: 'mortgage quotes dublin', 'mortgage advice dublin', 'mortgage broker dublin', 'mortgages dublin'.

Assessment: To appear in the top page of results, the website will need to be highly optimised. It will also need to be continually tweaked to retain and advance its position. This is an extremely competitive sector and the value of a lead is quite high. The geographic area is also relatively wide.

If you think SEO sounds complicated it should be borne in mind that there are large numbers of books that have been devoted just to this topic. You don't need to know everything about it - you just need to know what it can do for your business.

❸ Link Baiting and Blogging

You may come across some of the above terminology in your dealings with web design companies so here's a brief explanation:

→ 'Link baiting' is where you include content on your site that encourages other sites to link to it thus improving your search engine ranking position. For example, a bar might include a video that shows the perfect hot whiskey being made. Or a hotel might include a page that shows the top ten local attractions in the town.

→ Inserting a blog on your site is often advised at the web design stage. In some ways, a blog is just another form of link baiting but it also can be an access point (backdoor) to your website if the text included in the blog is particularly relevant to the search term. A blog is just a piece of text usually in the form of an article expressing an opinion or else providing useful information. Some bloggers will watch out for items that come up in the general news and then blog about them. For example, say your business is located in Limerick and a U.S. company announces a new factory. If you quickly blog about this new firm you are likely to get visitors to your website simply because so many people will be looking for information about this new company. The one obvious downside is that in most cases you will struggle to connect the news stories in a relevant and meaningful way to your actual business, but many business owners are just happy with the publicity a blog can bring.

❹ Search Engine Marketing (SEM)

SEM is used by some businesses to replace investment in SEO and by other businesses to supplement SEO investment.

SEM is often referred to as 'pay per click' advertising. This is because the most popular payment model involves you paying to have your advertisement displayed once a certain key word or phrase is input into a search engine. You are charged a variable fee only if the advertisement is clicked on. Usually these ads are displayed to the right of the normal search results or sometimes just above them. There are also options that allow your ad to appear on other third party sites that are interested in generating fee income from advertising.

Any business can easily run an SEM campaign. Each of the main search engines offers self-service options for business owners. The set up can be a little daunting but once you have run one campaign it gets much easier. There are limitations as to what you can include in your ad. There are a set number of letters and lines and there are also editorial guidelines that you must not breach or your ad will be refused.

Again, as with most areas of promotion, there are specialist companies willing to advise you and this can prove an attractive option for business owners who do not have the time to research this area fully.

Similar to SEO, there is a ranking system that decides which order the ads appear on the screen. Unlike SEO, money is the sole arbiter as to who finishes higher up the list. A somewhat complicated bidding system operates and the exact rules vary from one search engine to another. The bidding prices vary greatly depending on what is being advertised and the level of competition for the particular search term. For example, 'Lawyer Boston' might be a popular search term so the cost of appearing first on the ads might be quite high. However, 'probate Lawyer Boston' might have no competition and the cost per click might be minimal. Cost per click can vary from €0.10 to €7.00 and higher. 'Mortgages' and 'Mortgage brokers'

are traditionally seen as one of the most high cost search terms to be targeting.

From a budgeting perspective, there is huge flexibility with SEM in that you can set a monthly budget and then leave the search engine to manage it for you. At any time, you can increase or reduce your budget or simply postpone or cancel your campaign. Highly advanced analytical tools allow advertisers to drill down into a great level of detail to assess which campaigns and within that, which search terms are working best for them and delivering the best return on investment.

Panel 7.4

Getting the most out of SEM

Focus on the following:

→ Firstly, selecting the best search terms that will deliver the best value for your budget. You could select a strategy that targets just a few of the most popular search terms for your business or select a large number of less obvious ones. Or you could try a combination of both strategies.

→ Secondly, you need to ensure that your ads are sufficiently enticing that

(7.4 Continued)

when a potential customer sees the ad, that they are likely to click on it to see further information. This is not as easy as it sounds as most search engines limit your use of bold lettering, exclamation marks, duplicated wording and capitalisation.

SEM is an incredibly powerful form of advertising. It is often criticised because click-through rates tend to be poor compared to what can be achieved with SEO. But if no one clicks, you don't pay! What other advertising medium charges on this basis? Another criticism is that it is possible for competitors to click on your ads to try to make it more costly for you. The search engines have been working hard to reduce the effect of this and this is now less of a worry for advertisers. One of the key advantages is just how specific you can be with your message. It's amazing how creative you can be with such a small number of words to use.

With the vast majority of businesses not using SEM in any serious way, there is plenty of value left in this medium. It is unlikely to remain that way. In certain competitive sectors there is already evidence of some advertisers pulling back on their spend as the cost per click has risen sharply when the market has become more competitive. Each business needs to assess SEM on its merits to see what role it can play in your online marketing plans.

Panel 7.5

Sample SEM Ads

Riverside Bar & Grill
Early Bird Menu up to 7pm
2 courses only €15.95
www.riversidebargrill.com

Compare Mortgages Online
Compare 17 banks
Free consultation.
Apply online now!
www.abcmortgages.co.uk

Quick Tax Advice
Quick Expert Tax Advice
Locations nationwide
www.taxmeless.co.au

Baby Buggy Sale
10% off all online sales
Free delivery on first order
www.ForBaba.ie/buggies

❺ Banner Advertising

Large content-rich websites such as news websites and sports websites usually make most of their money by renting advertising space on their web pages. In most cases, the ads take the form of banner display ads. These are usually well designed, are in colour and increasingly many of these have some level of animated graphics.

Panel 7.6

Pricing Structures for Banner Ads

Many different pricing structures apply, but the four most common pricing mechanisms are as follows:

→ Cost per thousand page impressions (CPM) - this means that you pay a set price based on the number of people that are exposed to your ad.

→ Cost per click (CPC) - similar to SEM, you only pay based on who clicks on your ad.

→ Cost per acquisition (CPA) - this is where you pay based on the number of actual leads you generate. A tracking mechanism is built into this campaign to calculate how many of the people that clicked on your ad eventually completed an online enquiry form.

→ Fixed cost, usually per month. With this pricing mechanism you agree a fixed price with the website you are advertising on. The price is usually based on the audited number of page impressions that your ad is likely to appear on.

It is unlikely that you will have choice of payment mechanisms. At best, most websites will offer just two options and many offer only one. Other variables that decide the price are the size of the advertisement and the location on the page. As a general rule, larger news sites tend to attract big budget advertisers while smaller more niche sites tend to attract lower budget advertisers.

If you are considering banner advertising, you should consider what websites would it be best for you to associate with and then see what you can negotiate.

Panel 7.7

Banner Ads

❺ Social Media

Facebook, LinkedIn and Twitter are probably the most popular social networking sites currently operating. While they all operate in different ways and target different social groups, the common theme among them is that they each bring like-minded groups of people together in an online setting.

These sites also allow businesses to act as quasi-people. This means that you can set up an account for your business and then link up with other people who could then be exposed to your communication message. This is the first way that social networking sites can help your business. However, you as the business owner need to assess whether your inclusion on such a site is appropriate or value-adding for your business. Pubs, clubs and restaurants have probably got the most to gain while professional services firms such as accountants or lawyers have possibly the least. The best way to judge these sites is to sign up as an individual in order to see how they work.

The second way that these sites can be of value is through their advertising programs. Many of these sites operate 'pay per click' advertising options similar to those offered by the large search engines. Click through rates tend to be even lower than search engines but as you only pay for the clicks this is not so much of a worry. In fact, with Facebook, you can display your logo in an ad so even when you are not generating 'click throughs' to your website, you are still developing brand awareness - for free!

❻ Permission Marketing – E-Mail Marketing

This is the term that is used to describe marketing campaigns to consumers who have agreed to be marketed to. It is most often used in the context of e-mail marketing on the web.

Consumers are offered the opportunity to sign up to a regular newsletter or other communication via email. The website gradually builds a database of these 'friends' and communicates with them on a regular basis. This allows the business owner to build a relationship over time with groups of consumers who may then eventually become customers. It is a very low cost advertising method. There arc also quite a number of web-based software programs that allow you to manage these communications quite easily and also track their success rates.

❼ Information Marketing

While, strictly speaking, information marketing pre-dates the internet, it is the accessibility and low cost of the internet that has allowed it to take off in recent years.

Information Marketing can refer to the packaging of information that is then sold to a customer who needs the information. An example of this is someone producing an online downloadable guide to fly-fishing. Information marketing can also refer to situations where a company provides useful information (usually for free) that complements some of the products that it is selling. The thinking being that the company is establishing its credibility in a particular area in order that the customer might be more likely to purchase. An example would be a company selling surfboards publishing an online guide to the top ten surf locations.

❽ Offline Integration

It should also be noted that traditional 'offline' methods can and should be used to generate traffic to the company website. The website address should be included on company material including the following:

→ Stationery (business cards, compliment slips, headed paper, reports etc.)

→ Advertising (newspapers, TV, billboards)

→ Premises signage

→ Commercial vehicles

→ Promotional material (where possible).

"Traditional 'offline' methods can be used to generate traffic to your website"

The Growth of Online Marketing

What has gone before is a short crash course in online marketing methods. Online marketing continues to grow exponentially and it shows no signs of stopping. There are four key reasons behind the success of this medium:

→ The number of people using the internet and the amount of time they spend using it continues to grow each year.

→ It is much more targeted and customers and advertisers really like this. It gets away from more traditional methods which groups people into generic segments.

→ Consumers like the way that you can opt in and then easily opt out of permission marketing campaigns. This has built huge trust among web users.

→ Advertisers who invest the time in building their skills in online marketing benefit by seeing a much higher percentage of their advertising budgets being spent on actual advertising. With traditional methods, much of the budget can be swallowed up by advertising production costs thus making them more attractive to brands with larger advertising budgets.

Summary of Chapter 7

→ No website is often better than a bad website. Invest your money carefully

→ Don't stop at having a great website. Invest money in other ways to drive visitors to your website

→ Recognise the growth of online marketing and develop an understanding of what it can do for your business

→ Whatever marketing activities you engage in online, you should ensure that it is consistent with your offline marketing activities.

8

Appropriate Marketing Activities for Your Business

Chapter outline
Appropriate Marketing Activities for Your Business

→ Selecting the Most Appropriate Marketing Activities for Your Business
→ Monitoring Results
→ Advice on Promotion – When do You Need It?
→ Selecting External Advisers

❶ Selecting the Most Appropriate Marketing Activities for Your Business

There is clearly a wide range of ways that you can promote your business to potential customers. What you have to decide is which of the methods discussed in the earlier chapters best suit your particular business.

The starting point for this exercise is to look at your existing customer base. That should provide a basis by which you can identify the potential customer profiles that you are trying to target. Referring back to the principle of segmentation discussed in Chapter 2, these variables would include:

→ Age

→ Location

→ Gender

→ Socio-economic group

→ Job profile

→ Leisure interests

Following on from this you need to consider which promotional activity would best suit the selected profiles. A good way to do this is to rank each of the activities. See panel 8.1.

Panel 8.1

Issues for Consideration

When assessing a marketing activity you should consider each of the following issues:

→ How many people will see your message?

→ What percentage of these people are within your target market?

→ The capacity for the message to be noticed e.g. would the consumer be in the right frame of mind or will other promotional messages distract from your own message?

→ The cost of each activity. This should include all associated costs e.g. production costs.

→ Can any part of the activity be re-used at a lower cost later, e.g. a TV ad can be re-used?

→ The budget you have at your disposal.

→ The number of activities you wish to use. Using multiple activities tends to work better but only if the budget allows for an adequate spend in each area.

(8.1 Continued)

→ Are there specific advantages that particular activities might have, e.g. a promotional activity that operates close to the actual point of sale will tend to be more effective?

→ The production or service capacity you have within the business, e.g. some activities might produce a gradual uptake in new business over an extended period while others will produce a more short-term effect.

There is no proven formula to help you decide which promotional activities are best. The decisions in this area are normally based on the sound judgement of the business owner or their marketing adviser.

It is also worth considering all of your options. A common mistake is for a business to find a marketing program that 'pays for itself'. By this we mean that the cost of the program is at least covered by the profit generated by the program. This is a mistake because:

→ It usually fails to take into account the management time that has been invested into designing the program.

→ It usually does not take into account all of the staff resources utilised in generating the profit.

→ Most importantly, it does not allow for the other options that might have generated an even greater return on investment.

It is therefore critical that all costs be taken into account and that every possible method (within reason) is evaluated in advance.

❷ Combining Different Marketing Activities

There is considerable academic research and anecdotal evidence to show that where marketing activity is combined that the return on investment from each method is increased.

A typical example is where a company advertises a product on TV and also runs a series of newspaper ads at the same time. The recall or response rates to each campaign tend to be much higher.

There are various different maxims - mostly unscientific, but credible nonetheless - to back this up. For example, there is a 'rule of seven' that suggests a customer needs to see your brand/message seven times before they can really know your business and trust you enough to do business with you. Using multiple marketing activities can help you move more quickly to this point. This is perhaps one reason why Information Marketing is proving so effective.

MARKETING SKILLS: A PRACTICAL GUIDE

❸ Monitoring Results

Probably the greatest cardinal sin of marketers is not to monitor the results of campaigns. Small businesses tend to be the greatest sinners! Often the business owner's enthusiasm for the launch of the campaign is not matched by an enthusiasm to monitor the results.

Results need to be monitored in a very systematic way in order to assess the value of each campaign. This then feeds into future strategy.

It is not enough to have your telephonist tick off the number of phone calls that have been generated by a particular ad. The customer needs to be tracked from the initial enquiry right through to possible sale. The value of the sale needs to be recorded and any referral business also generated from that customer needs to be monitored also.

As mentioned above, you should always be in search of the best possible combination of marketing activities that provide optimum results for your business. Not just the activities that cover their own costs. This is an iterative, circular process that if managed correctly can pay handsome dividends for your business.

❹ Advice on Promotion – When do you need it?

In order to survive, some business owners often have to operate in a 'jack of all trades' type role. Depending on budget and time constraints, they often outsource some business functions. Finance or IT are usually the most likely functions to be outsourced.

Sales and marketing tend to be the least likely to be outsourced. The common sense reason for this is that many business owners know that they need to be able to sell in order to survive so the majority that are in business tend to have some skill in this area. Marketing is seen as a related discipline and because there are many common sense elements to marketing, many business owners are happy to take this role on themselves. And, many are very successful providing this role to their business. However, this is not always the case and many businesses underperform due to poor marketing effort.

Often the business owner's enthusiasm for the launch of the campaign is not matched by an enthusiasm to monitor the results.

Self-Awareness

It is important for business owners to have the self-awareness to judge how well they are performing when it comes to marketing. If at any point you feel you could be doing better then you may need to consider one or more of the following options:

→ Devoting more time to marketing your business

→ Upskilling yourself in areas where you consider yourself to be weak

→ Seeking advice from a specialist in the area.

Selecting External Advisers

The first two options in panel 8.2 are self explanatory so let's look at the latter of these three options. Many business owners are wary about taking on outside advice. The prime concern in most cases is the cost of this. This is a valid concern in that it can be very easy to spend over your budget.

Here are some practical ways how you can mitigate this risk:

→ Be absolutely clear as to the precise nature of the help you need, before you even consider contacting anyone.

→ Look at ways you can reduce cost by doing some of the more mundane parts of the project either yourself or by passing it to one of your own staff (e.g. you might outsource a DM campaign but run the mail merge and pack the envelopes in house).

→ Look at the types of advisers available and consider whether you need someone with broad experience (e.g. if you are planning a number of campaigns across multiple media) or a specialist adviser (e.g. if you have a requirement in a narrow area).

→ Draw up a shortlist of possible advisers and consider their previous experience and how it matches with your requirements.

→ When you select the adviser that you want to work with, you should draft a reasonably detailed brief and in turn request a written response to this as well as precise costings.

→ Ensure that you have enough time set aside in your own schedule to manage the project. This will ensure that you maximise the value of the adviser who most probably will be charging you on a per hour basis.

→ Tightly manage the project from start to finish.

→ Monitor the results and assess the value added by the adviser in order to inform future strategy.

Panel 8.3

Types of Advisers

→ General marketing consultancy

→ PR agency

→ Advertising agency

→ Media buying agency

→ Graphic designer

→ Website designer

→ Online marketing agency

→ Copywriting

→ Direct Marketing agency

Summary of Chapter 8

→ A deep understanding of who your key customers are provides the ideal platform for deciding which marketing activities to use

→ There is a considerable value in spreading your activity across various marketing activities

→ Monitoring results may be boring but it is critical in deciding future strategy

→ Just because a campaign 'pays for itself' doesn't mean it is effective

→ Seek advice where you need it but do some preparatory work to maximise the value of the advice.

Distribution

Chapter outline
Distribution

→ Building a Distribution Strategy
→ Levels of Distribution Intensity
→ Choosing the Correct
    Distribution Strategy
→ Online Distribution

❶ Building a Distribution Strategy

At its core Distribution is about getting the right amount of the right product to the right place at the right time and at the right price. By doing this well it has the propensity to add value to the other elements of the marketing mix; if it fails to deliver in any of those functions it undermines the marketing effort.

Suppliers choose to link with customers through channels mostly because doing so increases their reach and puts them into markets they could not economically service themselves. But outside of that basic logistic concern there are many other questions to consider. See panel 9.1.

Panel 9.1

Distribution - Key Considerations

→ **The Target Market** - the first consideration has to be what the customer wants. Where and how do they want to purchase? What level, or intensity of, distribution coverage is needed to meet their needs? How much interaction with the seller might they require, for instance, to fine tune their purchase or find out more about the product?

→ **Channel management** - what resources are you prepared to put into the management of your distribution channel links to cater for:

- **Brand support** - to what extent are the links in the distribution chain required to preserve/enhance the image of the product? Purveyors of luxury goods will select 'resellers' very

carefully, often on an exclusive basis; suppliers of fast moving consumer goods, while keeping some control of merchandising at the outlet, will be more focussed on 'footfall'. Poor performance by resellers, whether in the handling of the product or interacting with customers will erode brand value.

- **Sales support** - what degree of selling-on of your offer is demanded at channel level? What level of product knowledge or technical expertise does this imply and what initial and ongoing costs (e.g. on training, on sales support material) are to be budgeted to ensure this?

For example in the PC market, the likes of the PC World chain provide

(9.1 Continued)

expertise at the retail level that appeals to people who may not feel they have the technical savvy or confidence to specify their exact requirements on a Dell website.

- **Feedback** - the people who bring your offer a step nearer your customer can be a vital source of market information/research. They can pass on their assessment of customer satisfaction, ideas for product enhancement and intelligence on competitor performance/planned moves.

- **Performance management** - what resources can be

committed to managing goals and quality in the chain? For example, decisions on adding or deleting members and assessing how these actions may impact on existing members of the channel?

→ **Partnership** - how close do you bring channel participants to you? How involved in mapping development will they be?

→ **Risk carrying and Incentivisation** - what level of financial risk do you ask channel members to carry? Financing arrangements? Commission, discounts, rebates?

❷ Levels of Distribution Intensity

There are basically three levels of distribution intensity:

→ Mass distribution - means getting the product into all outlets/retail stores where the category is sold in the area (supermarkets, convenience stores, petrol stations). Fast moving consumer goods are the prime example. A given chocolate bar, for example, must be merchandised effectively on those display counters because, if not, the customer has a range of other

choices in the same category. The costs of supporting this intensity of distribution are high, so high turnover is essential. Feedback from the reseller is essentially quantitative - the numbers do the talking.

→ Selective distribution - using a more limited selection of outlets in a geographic area to reach a customer group who are more likely to seek the product out than expect it to be available everywhere. The relationship between the supplier and the reseller will be closer in terms of inputs, such as training, from the former and more active 'selling' from the latter. Likely to be the route selected by producers of consumer durables, particularly at the higher price points. Feedback is both qualitative and quantitative.

→ Exclusive distribution - takes the selective option to another level where delivery is confined to just one wholesaler, distributor or retailer in a given geographic sector. This option is essentially the domain of high-end products with a well established and strong brand position. The supplier can rely on a carefully chosen partner to preserve and even enhance that image; the reseller can count on the brands discerning clientele beating a path to his door. Detailed qualitative feedback is available to the supplier.

❸ Choosing the correct Distribution Strategy

Small business owners often make the assumption that the greater the level of distribution for your product, the greater your profit. In most cases, the exact opposite is true. In addition, too broad a distribution strategy usually shortens the life span of your product. Why is this? Two reasons:

→ Firstly, the pursuit of a mass distribution strategy exhausts management resources. The

effect of this is to dilute the level of success despite the huge investment in time. However, most small business owners are able to recognise this at some point in the evolution of the business and take corrective action.

→ Secondly, a mass distribution strategy can ruin your well thought out pricing strategy. Look at this example. You sell your product to resellers at €8.00. Reseller A takes your product and sells it at the recommended retail price of €12.95. Reseller B offers the product at €10.95 to beat the competitor. Reseller C is an online seller with a lower cost base and sells the product at €9.95. Resellers A and B continue in a downward spiral in pricing until your resellers' margin is seriously eroded. With a limited margin in your product, orders begin to dry up. Your product dies.

The alternative strategy is of course to pursue a selective or exclusive distribution strategy. Both these strategies, offer the advantages of a lower investment in management time and a much greater control on your product pricing. You have much more power to set pricing where distribution is being limited to a select group. The decision you have to take is whether these two advantages can outweigh the advantages of having the greater exposure for your product that mass distribution brings.

The key consideration here is that decisions with regard to distribution can appear easy but this is not always the case and the relative merits of all of the various strategies should be weighed carefully when finalising your business plan.

❹ Online Distribution

The internet has transformed the way many products and services are distributed. Many business have used the internet to complement existing channels of distribution while new businesses have emerged that use the internet as the sole method of distribution.

The obvious attractions of the internet as a distribution channel include:

→ Low costs

→ Relatively easy to manage

→ Highly scaleable

→ Ability to reach international markets with relative ease.

The decision for business owners is to identify whether there is a place for the internet within the overall distribution strategy and if so, how to best take advantage of this.

The internet also offers huge opportunities for businesses to outsource non-core elements of the sales process and this can be very attractive for new or start-up businesses. These elements include:

→ The customer interface - there are many ready made 'shops' and other customer interfaces that save you having to build your own

→ Payment systems - you can acquire a merchant account from one of many companies who are willing to manage online payments on your behalf

→ Customer communications - other firms offer a facility whereby you can easily outsource regular marketing communications to your existing customers

→ Order fulfilment - why worry about stocking product in your own warehouse when you can outsource this to a company specialising in order fulfilment?

Let's look at a real life example: A business owner launches a new product that is aimed at golfers. The product is manufactured in China. The business owner decides to use the internet as the only distribution method. The front end customer interface is outsourced to eBay (using the Shop functionality within eBay), the payment facility is outsourced to PayPal, the online payments specialists, the order fulfilment, warehousing of the product and delivery of the product are outsourced to a specialist logistics firm. As you can see the business owner's main tasks are marketing the business and managing the various outsourced arrangements. This type of model can free up more management time that in turn would be devoted to the design or acquisition of new product lines.

There is one last practical point to be made about the internet and its role in distribution strategy. Business owners should not dismiss or ignore the internet simply because they don't understand enough about it. This is almost certainly the road to, at best, underperformance and at worst, the demise of your business. Try to hire staff that can fill in knowledge gaps in relation to the internet or else buy in advice from outside consultants.

Summary of Chapter 9

→ Distribution is about :

  - Right product, right place, right time, right price

→ Mass distribution may not be as attractive as it sounds - results may not justify the costs of achieving this reach

→ A Selective or Exclusive approach can be a better fit for SMEs

→ Managing the chosen channels is vital

→ Be careful not to ignore the potential advantages of an online distribution strategy.

10 Building for the Future

Chapter outline
Building for the Future

→ The Dynamics of Your Business
→ The Porter Model
  - Threat of New Entrants
  - Threat of Substitution
  - Bargaining Power of Buyers
  - Competitive Rivalry
→ Strategies that Emerge from the Model
→ The Customer's Value Chain

❶ The Dynamics of Your Business

Businesses, caught up in the imperatives of the 'now' - how to get the new offer to market effectively, what response do we have to a competitor's new prices? - often fail to take account of the many powerful forces acting on them from outside. These influences can be game-breakers so, before getting down to the business of outperforming the competition, it is vital that a company takes time to look at the dynamics of their situation. There are many ways of approaching this, but we are going to look at an approach that has been tried and tested and works for SME's as well as it does for large corporations. The value will come from a pragmatic application of the parts that you see best fit your company, rather than a too-rigid interpretation.

❷ The Porter Model

Porter's Five Forces: Michael Porter's model suggests that the profitability of an industry is determined by five forces (See panel 10.1)

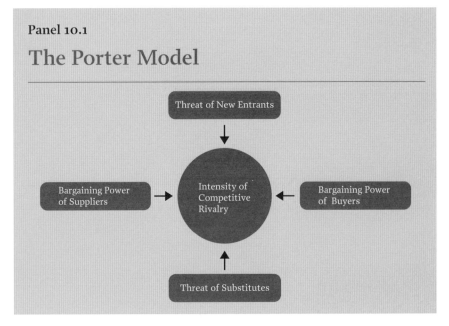

Panel 10.1

The Porter Model

As has been pointed out above, too often businesses concentrate primarily on the central arena here, the Competitive Rivalry, which they naturally see as the main battleground, ignoring or paying little heed to the other forces. But it is vitally important to have an understanding of how the four external forces can have an impact. We will look at each of these forces in turn.

Threat of New Entrants

Put basically, if there are <u>no, or very low barriers to entry</u> into your business, then you should not expect to do well for long without others seeking to get in on the act. So a company needs to look to where there are barriers that would discourage new entrants, barriers that it may be possible to build or reinforce.

→ **Brand:** Do you have a brand presence, or can you build one, that could act as a deterrent? A strong brand presence, established over time in a market is a discouragement to potential new entrants.

→ **Distribution:** Do you have, or can you engineer, some unique angles on access to distribution? Some pharmaceutical distributors, for instance, have forged strong links with chemists.

→ **Inputs:** Do you have, or can you engineer, some unique angles on access to inputs/suppliers?

→ **Know how:** Have you 'proprietary knowledge' - some part of the business process in which you have learned/invented unique ways of doing things that are not easily copied? Software Developers specialising in niche market segments are an example.

→ **Expected retaliation:** Do you send out clear signals that you will respond vigorously to incursions?

Threat of Substitution

Buyers: Do your buyers have a propensity to switch? Do you really know where you impact in their Value Chain? We will further develop this topic in this chapter.

Evolution of Distribution Channels: An example would be the impact of online airline booking on travel agents. Do you watch for potential new ways of delivering to your markets?

Technology: Do you keep a close eye on developments in other industries - new materials being used, new processes that parallel yours?

Bargaining Power of Buyers

Concentration: Are your buyers few in numbers and liable to cooperate in pushing for deals, or are they dispersed?

Backward Integration: Are you supplying so much of what they do (and seen to be making a profit from it) that they might be tempted to take it on themselves?

Bargaining Power of Suppliers

Concentration: Are they few in numbers and liable to cooperate, or dispersed and less likely to pose this threat? Should you look at spreading your net a bit wider?

Forward Integration: Is their input into your business (in which they see you making profit) so significant that they might be tempted to get in on the act? If so should you look at diversifying your sources?

Competitive Rivalry

It is only when we have had a good look at what impact all of the above forces can have on your business and how we might adjust things to your advantage, that we look at the main stage, the arena of Competitive Rivalry. At this point we can now move to the question of how you find some sort of sustainable advantage over those competing with you for market space.

To start with it is useful to look at what we know about the dynamics of the marketplace - what are the things that generate competitive heat?

For instance what is the growth rate of the industry you are in? If it is at the early stage of fast growth, that is the time we should be looking to gain share, as competitors are less likely to notice or even worry. Gaining share is also important because this is the phase that 'me too' competition is likely to jump in. As industry growth levels off into the more modest annual rate of a mature market, the arena of competitive rivalry becomes more demanding. The rising tide is no longer lifting all boats. Most markets are in this mature phase. Much of this book deals with how to manage marketing in this setting.

We should also be conscious, for our marketing focus, of the effect that the share structure

of the market we are in has on competitive intensity. A market with one dominant player and a scattering of followers with small shares will typically generate less heat than one in which leadership fluctuates, year by year, amongst a few relatively evenly matched rivals. Having a good picture of the game we are in enables us to play it better.

❸ Strategies that emerge from the Model

At this point let us take it that the Five Forces model has been used to give us a good working analysis of the market environment we are in and ask, given that picture as background, where to from here?

Porter contends that there are really only three generic strategies that can successfully deliver competitive advantage; Low Cost, Differentiation or Focus. See panel 10.2. While it is true that their application may be more easily understood in the context of business to business, they can also apply to consumer marketing.

Five Forces model has been used to give us a good working analysis of the market environment we are in and ask, given that picture as background, where to from here?

Panel 10.2

Sources of Competitive Advantage

		Low cost	Differentiation
Breadth of Target	Broad	Overall cost leadership	Differentation
	Segment(s)	Focus	Focus

Low Cost Strategy

The first of these, Low Cost, which involves opening up a significant and sustainable cost advantage over competitors, is not likely to be an option for many of our audience. The other two, however, are typically where good SME's operate.

The Differentiation Strategy

This approach says that what is needed is for a company to select one or more characteristics that are widely valued by buyers (see Value Chain below) and then to achieve and sustain superior performance in those than any competitor.

Achieving this will allow the company to charge premium prices, which, in turn, lead to above average profitability (assuming cost parity or proximity).

Differentiation requires:

→ Strong marketing skills to carry the 'proposition' to the customer

→ Good coordination between functions in the company - all 'on message'

→ A corporate reputation for quality

→ Cooperative distribution to ensure the offer is not degraded along the line.

The Focus Strategy

This alternative requires that a company narrows down its focus to a segment (or a couple of segments) within the industry and then seeks to target those segments exclusively. Optimising strategy for those targets means achieving cost leadership or differentiation for the target(s), though not overall.

Focus requires:

→ A keen sense of how the overall market is broken down

→ Most of the same requirements as for differentiation.

The message to be underscored is that many firms do not have competitive advantage because they have only bits and pieces of the generic strategies and thus they fall between stools. It is, of course possible to excel in a couple of the generic strategies. Amazon, for instance, has achieved Cost Leadership in book distribution with an IT enabled supply chain. They hold relatively little stock, but can have an item delivered rapidly from their network. At the same time they are Differentiated from the traditional bookstore in the way they offer the customer a very powerful search engine to comb their huge database. We can also see that Toyota, while being a Cost Leader in the making of automobiles, offers a clear example of Differentiation with the Prius Hybrid.

The most profitable strategy can change as industries evolve, e.g. through innovation in processes, or Supply Chain modifications. Crucially, the best generic strategy is influenced by and evolves to take account of competitors' strategies as they change.

❹ The Customer's Value Chain

This is a template for examining how and where the generic strategies might apply. Again it may be easier to see this in a B2B context than consumer, though it equally applies with the latter. What this method does is to break up what your customer does into strategically relevant activities:

So, the task is to describe what it is they do under the headings below and then ask, where can we have a positive impact in there by either:

→ Lowering their costs/improving efficiency?

→ Improving their performance vis-à-vis their customers?

It pre-supposes a very detailed understanding of what your customer does.

Any business can be broken up into the following sequence of steps:

→ Inbound - they buy in products and/or services. The better these meet their procurement processes (payment, quality assurance, storage, cost control etc.) the happier they are with that supplier.

→ Operations - they do things with these purchases. They engage in assembly or processing to add value. The easier the purchased goods or services fit with their operations (e.g. by speeding them up, reducing costs/downtime, exceeding quality requirements), so much the better for the position of the supplier and the longer term relationship.

→ Outbound - they package, store and deliver onwards their own value proposition. Can your input help at this point, e.g. by way of shelf life, ruggedness etc?

→ Marketing and Sales - can the inclusion of a known and

valued brand within their offer enhance their marketing efforts (e.g. in the way that Dell advertise that their PCs run with Intel microchips)?

→ Service - they back up all of this with after sales service, help desks or websites. Can you in some way supplement this effort (e.g. providing your own support service to assist with some queries/technical problems)?

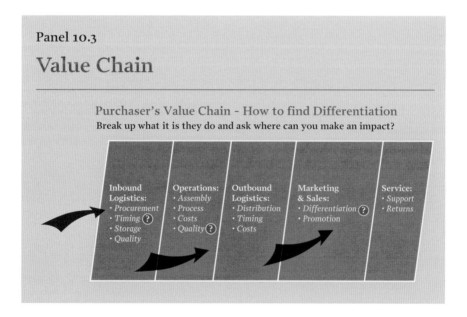

Panel 10.3

Value Chain

Purchaser's Value Chain - How to find Differentiation
Break up what it is they do and ask where can you make an impact?

Summary of Chapter 10

→ The Five Forces Model can be used to map the dynamics of your industry and;

→ It can be a powerful generator of strategic options

→ Dissect the nature of your customer's needs, using the Value Chain approach, to assess where you can make the best impact.

Notes

Notes

Notes

Notes

Notes

Notes

Notes

Further publications in 2011 and 2012

- → Managing Reward
- → Handling Discipline - *Best Practice*
- → Managing Diversity
- → Negotiating Skills
- → Burnout
- → Coaching Skills
- → Life Balance
- → Conflict Resolution
- → Influencing Skills
- → Mediation Skills
- → Assertiveness and Self-Esteem
- → Strategic Issue Communications
- → Personal Development
- → Innovation
- → Compliance
- → Strategy Development and Implementation
- → Leadership and Strategic Change
- → Managing with Impact - *Focusing on Performance through People*
- → Strategic Marketing
- → Entrepreneurial Skills
- → Managing Attendance at Work
- → Employee Relations
- → Improving your Writing Skills
- → Organisation Development/ Training
- → Change Management
- → Organisation Design
- → Energy Management
- → International Marketing
- → Governance in Today's Corporate World
- → Customer Relationship Management
- → Building Commitment to Quality
- → Understanding Finance
- → PR Skills for Managers
- → Logistics and Supply Chain
- → Dealing with Difficult People
- → Effective Meetings
- → Communication Skills
- → Facilitation Skills
- → Managing Upwards
- → Giving and Receiving Feedback
- → Consumer Behaviour
- → Delegation and Empowerment
- → Basic Economics for Managers
- → Finance for non Financial Executives
- → Business Forecasting
- → The Marketing of Services

Management Briefs
Essential Insights for Busy Managers

Our list of books already published includes:

→ Be Interview-Wise: *How to Prepare for and Manage* <u>*Your*</u> *Interviews*
Brian McIvor

→ HR for Line Managers: *Best Practice*
Frank Scott-Lennon & Conor Hannaway

→ Bullying & Harassment: *Values and Best Practice Responses*
Frank Scott-Lennon & Margaret Considine

→ Career Detection: *Finding and Managing Your Career*
Brian McIvor

→ Impactful Presentations: *Best Practice Skills*
Yvonne Farrell

→ Project Management: *A Practical Guide*
Dermot Duff & John Quilliam

→ Marketing Skills: *A Practical Guide*
Garry Hynes & Ronan Morris

→ Performance Management: *Developing People and Performance*
Frank Scott-Lennon & Fergus Barry

→ Proven Selling Skills: *For Winners*
Ronan McNamara

→ Redundancy: *A Development Opportunity for You!*
Frank Scott-Lennon, Fergus Barry & Brian McIvor

→ Safety Matters!: *A Guide to Health & Safety at Work*
Adrian Flynn & John Shaw of Phoenix Safety

→ Time Matters: *Making the Most of Your Day*
Julia Rowan

→ Emotional Intelligence (EQ): *A Leadership Imperative!*
Daire Coffey & Deirdre Murray